Come to the Waters

Also by Diane Head . . .

A Precious Bit of Forever

Come to the Waters

Meditations for Thirsty Moms

DIANE HEAD

Zondervan Publishing House
Grand Rapids, Michigan

Daybreak Books are published by Zondervan Publishing House, 1415 Lake Drive, S.E., Grand Rapids, Michigan 49506.

COME TO THE WATERS
Copyright © 1985 by The Zondervan Corporation
Grand Rapids, Michigan

Library of Congress Cataloging in Publication Data

Head, Diane, 1945-
   Come to the waters.

   1. Mothers—Prayer-books and devotions—English.
I. Title.
BV4847.H43   1985   242'.6431   84–25609
ISBN 0-310-25941-X

Unless otherwise indicated, Scripture quotations are from the *New American Standard Bible*. Scripture quotations marked (LB) are from *The Living Bible*. Copyright © 1971 by Tyndale House Publishers, Wheaton, Ill. Used by permission. Scripture quotations marked (NIV) are from the HOLY BIBLE: NEW INTERNATIONAL VERSION (North American Edition). Copyright © 1978 by the International Bible Society. Used by permission of Zondervan Bible Publishers.

Edited by Kin Millen and Julie Ackerman Link

Printed in the United States of America

85 86 87 88 89 / 10 9 8 7 6 5 4 3 2

For Amy Beth

Come, all you who are thirsty,
*   come to the waters;*
and you who have no money,
*   come, buy and eat!*
Come, buy wine and milk
*   without money and without cost.*
Why spend money on what is not bread,
*   and your labor on what does not satisfy?*
Listen, listen to me, and eat what is good,
*   and your soul will delight in the richest of fare.*
                                    (Isaiah 55:1–2 NIV)

Contents

Special thanks to my family:

To Robert, my husband and best friend, for his loving encouragement;

To Melinda and Amy for their love, patience, and help
during the hours I spent with a typewriter attached to my fingers.

His Rest

Come to Me, all who are weary and heavy-laden, and I will give you rest (Matthew 11:28).

Do you ever feel as though you have nothing left to give? That so many demands are made of you that you've become depleted . . .

empty . . .

exhausted?

Do you have an automatic signal when your posterior hits the bottom of a chair—immediately a voice from the farthest room in the house calls "MOTHER . . . " as if the house were on fire?

If you answered a hearty "amen" to the above, congratulations. You're a bonafide member of twentieth century motherhood. One of the conditions of membership is that you exchange your calm and orderly life for upheaval, busyness, and whirlwind activity.

We entered motherhood so eagerly—babes in our arms and stars in our eyes. So cuddly and cute, these wee ones took hold of our hearts and lives. We didn't know the gentle thump, thump, thump of their hearts was the ticking of a time bomb, ready to explode with the energy of an atomic bomb at any minute. As parents, we are the managers and harnessers of this energy, so we fill our days with clever schemes and fancy plans to keep our children occupied. Soon we find ourselves caught in the great carpool of life. We pick up and drop off mini-ballerinas, soccer players, piano virtuosos, and future NFL champions until life is little more than a blur.

Twentieth-century motherhood also offers its members . . .

The mental stimulation of hunting for dirty laundry.

Fun-filled hours collecting papers for the school paperdrive.

The thrill of finding the third stepped-on retainer in one month.

The unequalled satisfaction of matching two dozen like-colored socks of varying sizes.

The opportunity to practice small motor skills and develop mental dexterity by braiding hair, calling PTA members about the cookie sale, and planning the supper menu—all while loudly tapping out the beat for your budding trumpeter.

The challenge of camoflaging the Hot-Wheels tracks through the new pansy bed.

The joy of creatively redecorating the house in handprint hues and smudge-colored wallpaper.

Whoever said today's mother doesn't "work"? There is no doubt about it—ours is a full-time, emotionally and physically draining occupation. No time off. No paid vacations. Plenty of overtime.

If ever anyone needed rest, it's today's mother. And I have great news. There *is* rest for us—a rest more rejuvenating than a long and leisurely nap, and more soothing to frayed nerves than a Brahms concert. This rest reaches into the depths of our souls and claims us from within.

This special promise of rest comes from Jesus' words in Matthew 11:29: "Take my yoke upon you and learn of me . . . and you shall find rest" (KJV). The yoke spoken of in this passage is fashioned of discipline and discipleship; its lining is love. Rather than bringing restriction, it brings refreshment. Through this yoke He calls us to learn of Himself and find quietness and blessed rest.

Rest for the soul is the most desirable rest. It affects not only our spiritual health, but our emotional and physical health as well. The only way to receive this rest is to sit at Christ's feet and hear His word, to take the time to learn more about who He is and what He is like.

"Oh, dear," you may say, "there is so little time in my day for *me*. Alone. By myself. Unbusy. And if I can't find time even for myself, how in the world am I going to find time to learn of God?"

Wait a minute . . . could it be that our priorities are upside down?

> *We are wives*
> *We are mothers*
>> *But first we are God's beloved*
>>> *Created to know Him*
>>> *Created to respond to that knowledge with love.*

Just as it takes *time* for two people to get to know each other and to build a loving friendship, it takes *time* to build a love-relationship with God.

And how can we get to know Him better? Only through the disciplined use of our time, time spent prayerfully reading and meditating on His Word. For it is through His Word that He speaks to us of Himself and reveals exactly what He is like through the person of Jesus Christ (John 14:9). Love for Him will grow from our knowledge of His character.

However, our dilemma is still with us. The demands for our time are tremendous during these parenting years. It may seem like an impossibility to plan time alone with God, but with His help and a bit of determination it can be done. It *must* be done.

Some of us may have success with early morning devotions, even though it's often a struggle to roust out of bed in a race with an early, pre-dawn riser. And it may take a bit of explanation to our husbands when we doze over dinner, but the *rest* to our souls will far outweigh the missed sleep; when we manage morning devotions, our days are blessed with serenity, confidence, and power that come from beginning in His presence.

But morning devotions aren't for *everyone*. Many of us have nights with fussy babies or sick kids, or our husbands work strange hours, so some of us may have to use our creativity to find valuable moments alone with God. These moments will probably come in different places and at different times each day. Moments alone with Him may only come as we're waiting for the carpool kids or nursing the baby in the middle of the night. The place and time aren't important. He is as much with us while we stand in front of our stoves as He is when we kneel beside our beds.

It is amazing that the King of Kings, the Lord of Lords, the almighty God and

Creator of all things wants you and me to know Him better. He wants to open His heart to us. He actually delights in our knowledge of Him!

> I don't want your sacrifices—I want your love;
> I don't want your offerings—I want you to know me.
>
> (Hosea 6:6 LB)

He waits expectantly for you . . . for me. He waits for us to make the time to meet Him . . . to learn of Him and find rest for our souls.

From the still waters of His presence . . . from the wellspring of His riches . . . we can joyously draw precious, thirst-quenching water.

> *To be filled to overflowing,*
> *like a watered garden . . . a spring of water*
> *whose waters do not fail.*

> The LORD will guide you always;
> he will satisfy your needs in a sun-scorched land
> and will strengthen your frame.
> You will be like a well-watered garden,
> like a spring whose waters never fail.
>
> (Isaiah 58:11 NIV).

Come to the waters!

Blessed Father, we praise You for the rest You provide in Your presence. You refresh us. You revive us. You restore us—abundantly! Thank You for the special joy that is ours during these precious moments alone with You.

amen

His Presence

> *Where can I go from your Spirit?*
> *Where can I flee from your presence?*
> *If I go to the heavens, you are there;*
> *if I make my bed in the depths, you are there.*
> *If I rise on the wings of the dawn,*
> *if I settle on the far side of the sea,*
> *even there your hand will guide me,*
> *your right hand will hold me fast.*
>
> *(Psalm 139:7–10 NIV)*

Mommy, how can God be listening to me if He is taking care of everyone else's prayers at the same time?" my five-year-old Amy asked one night during bedtime prayers.

How do I explain God's omnipresence to a child? I thought to myself. *The wonder of it is even too great for me to comprehend. Do I tell her God is spirit; therefore, His love and His power cannot be contained in any one place, whether it be heaven or earth? He is totally present everywhere! He even says to us, "Do I not fill heaven and earth?"* (Jeremiah 23:24 NIV). *How can a child begin to understand?*

So I said simply, "God is so wonderful and great that He can be everywhere at once. Everywhere you go He is with you. Right now and always. He has all the time in the world—just for *you!* When you talk to Him it's as if you were sitting on His lap and He had nothing else to do except hold you and talk with you."

Amy looked up at me with shining eyes. "Wow, Mommy! He must really love me."

Oh, for the faith and acceptance of a child! As adults our faith can get all scrambled up with our feelings. If we're tired or irritable God seems as far away as the most distant star . . . and our prayers don't seem to get beyond the lowest ceiling. It's as if His presence is dependent upon our mental and emotional state.

We also have a tendency to project our own weaknesses upon God. For example, hard as we try, we aren't always available to those who need us. Could God be like that too? Maybe *He's* just too busy. Perhaps He has something or someone more important to attend to before He can give us the attention we need.

These are our feelings. But don't despair. There is never a moment when we and our concerns are out of His thoughts!

> Can a mother forget the baby at her breast
>   and have no compassion on the child she has borne?
> Though she may forget,
>   I will not forget you!
> See, I have engraved you on the palms of my hands;
>   your walls are ever before me.
>
> (Isaiah 49:15–16 NIV)

Even before we know we need His attention, heaven's door of eternal immediacy swings open wide. Our Lord has all the time in eternity for us—*individually!* Each of us is as much alone with Him this moment as if we were His only child.

> We all have those days when we're
>   weary of household chores
>   discouraged with a money shortage
>   afraid of our kids' tomorrows
>   doubting God's timing
>   angry at being taken for granted

lonely because no one seems to understand.

Let's tell Him.

When our anxious thoughts threaten to overwhelm us—His consolations will delight our souls. "Lord, when doubts fill my mind, when my heart is in turmoil, quiet me and give me renewed hope and cheer" (Psalm 94:19 LB).

It is a communion of the highest order. Open. Honest. Soul-baring. Communion with an ever-present God. We belong to a God who hears our every cry even before it is uttered. What greater soul-calming balm can there be!

He is with us through each moment of joy . . . or sorrow. He surrounds each of those moments with Himself . . . with peace.

Let us therefore draw near with confidence to the throne of grace, that we
may receive mercy and find grace to help in time of need.

(Hebrews 4:16)

Father, thank You for Your great and glorious presence in our lives. We praise You for having time for us—for Your total availability each moment of our days. We can almost hear You whisper, "I am here, my child. Come to Me." We come with hearts of joy!

amen

His Comfort

He tends his flock like a shepherd:
He gathers the lambs in his arms
and carries them close to his heart;
he gently leads those that have young.

(Isaiah 40:11 NIV)

One of the sweetest memories of motherhood is the precious experience of breast-feeding. What joy to pick up my tiny, red-faced, wailing bundle and hold her close where she found comfort and nourishment. I cuddled her and whispered to her. She felt the rhythm of my heart. She enjoyed the warmth of my arms. Her world once again became secure as she sleepily relaxed deep in my love.

God offers us the same kind of security. His very name invites us to seek comfort and nourishment in Him. One of the Old Testament names for God is *El-Shaddai*—a name of mighty promise and all-sufficient power. However, it has another meaning of deeper intimacy, of special significance to us as mothers.

The word from which Hebrew scholars believe *Shaddai* is derived is translated *breast*. With this translation in mind, *Shaddai* means "One who nourishes, supplies, and satisfies." By adding the Hebrew word for God, *El,* the name becomes *One mighty to nourish, satisfy, and supply.* What a beautiful description of our God! Not simply a name— but the very essence of His being. He comforts us as only a mother can.

> For thus says the Lord, "Behold, I extend peace to her like a river,
> And the glory of the nations like an overflowing stream;
> And you shall be nursed, you shall be carried on the hip and fondled on
>   the knees.
> As one whom his mother comforts, so I will comfort you."
>   (Isaiah 66:12–13)

This portrait of God brings an image of Jesus to mind. Picture Him sitting on a grassy knoll, the Sea of Galilee sparkling in the distance, birds soaring above in a hot and clear sky, the crowds hushed as He gathers the little children into His arms. Imagine being a child on that day . . .

> *Climbing up on His lap . . .*
> *Looking deep in His eyes . . .*
> *Feeling the strength of His arms holding you close—so close . . .*
> *You can feel the rough warmth of His robe and hear the rhythm of His*
>   *heart.*

What delight! What joy it would have been! Wait a minute . . . *would have been?* What about right now?

Is this a childish, unsophisticated image of our God? No. This same Jesus *is El-Shaddai.*

God became man and lived in our world. He lived in a family with children who giggled and yelled. He worked with His hands. He felt hot and tired. He felt pain. He felt joy. He felt sadness. He laughed. He cried. *Just like us.*

Because He knows what it's like to be human—to suffer, to hurt—His comfort somehow touches us with deeper meaning. He has been here, in the middle of life's roughest waters. Nothing takes Him by surprise.

Are we hurting from someone's broken promise? Are we deeply wounded from a sharp or thoughtless word? Are we aching right along with a suffering child, a discouraged husband, or a troubled friend?

He knows what it's like.
He feels every heartache.

Nothing touches our lives that hasn't touched Him first, that hasn't hurt Him first. Every angry word spoken to us has been spoken to Him. Each pain and each sorrow has pierced His heart before.

He understands. Because He understands, His comfort knows no limit. We can take deep consolation from the knowledge of His providing presence. But how can we take nourishment from Him?

Praise God! In His wisdom and understanding of our humanity, particularly the need to grasp hold of something far more real than feelings, He has given us an unending source of nourishment. It springs forth as a river, flowing directly from Him . . . ancient yet forever new, unchanging yet forever relevant. A source of wisdom, strength, and joy. The eternal, living, and holy Word of God!

Each word written there proceeds from the very mouth of our God directly to us, His own. His Word is the vehicle He uses to transport us straight into His arms. With His Word He speaks to us, saying, " . . . I have summoned you by name; you are Mine! . . . You are precious and honored in my sight, and . . . I love you" (Isaiah 43:1–5).

I am with you and will watch over you wherever you go (Genesis 28:15).
I myself will help you (Isaiah 41:14).
I will take hold of your hand. I will keep you (Isaiah 42:6).
I, even I, am He who comforts you (Isaiah 51:12).
I will go before you and will level the mountains (Isaiah 45:2).
I have loved you with an everlasting love (Jeremiah 31:3).

We are fed.
We are comforted.
We are held
　　　　in His arms.

Our blessed Lord ... our El-Shaddai, thank You for understanding us—no matter how deep or painful our heartache. Somehow Your comfort is greater because You know—and have experienced—our feelings. You console and gladden our hearts—we can't help but praise and adore You, our Father!

amen

His Gifts

For the Lord God is a sun and shield;
the Lord bestows favor and honor;
no good thing does He withhold
from those whose walk is blameless.

(Psalm 84:11 NIV)

Do you ever gaze longingly at the house up on the hill? The one with at least six bathrooms and the trees with leaves that refuse to fall on the lawn?

Do you sigh when a new luxury car passes you on the freeway—as you rattle along in economy-sized practicality, your subcompact generously bedecked with fingerprints, toys, and cookie crumbs?

"Ah, it must be nice to enjoy such wealth," you sigh.

Then along comes a smudgy hug and a freckle-faced grin and suddenly you feel very rich.

Wealth? What is it really? We all have different ideas about it. Some of us pursue, or simply wish for, material wealth. Others of us seek intellectual wealth. Some of us think of physical beauty, strength, or shapeliness as the measuring stick of wealth.

When I find my eyes are being drawn toward Madison Avenue riches it's time to take inventory of the wealth that is mine, wealth of far more real, and enduring—even eternal—value.

The greatest gift God has given us is our relationship with Him through His Son, Jesus Christ. He gives us forgiveness. He calls us His friend. His beloved. His lamb. His treasured possession. What joy is ours to have a love-relationship like this with our sovereign God—our Creator! He sacrificed His only son to save you—to save me—to restore us to Himself. In light of this gift alone, we are the wealthiest of all people!

And His gifts don't end here. He gives us eternal life. We will be with Him in a place He has prepared especially for us. Talk about wealth! If we don't recognize it now—we certainly will then.

Then there are the treasures He pours out upon us: strength and peace (Psalm 29:11); favor and honor (Psalm 84:11); wisdom, knowledge, and joy (Ecclesiastes 2:26); everything we need for life and godliness (2 Peter 1:3).

Wealth? How could we ask for more? But we do, and that's good. He wants us to ask in accordance with His character and objectives:

> In that day you will no longer ask me anything. I tell you the truth, my Father will give you whatever you ask in my name. Until now you have not asked for anything in my name. Ask and you will receive, and your joy will be complete.
>
> (John 16:23–24)

> Ask and it will be given to you; seek and you will find; knock and the door will be opened to you. For everyone who asks receives; he who seeks finds; and to him who knocks, the door will be opened. . . . If you, then, though you are evil, know how to give good gifts to your children, how much more will your Father in heaven give good gifts to those who ask him!
>
> (Matthew 7:7–8, 11)

Isn't it wonderful that God has allowed us to enjoy not only His spiritual gifts, but also physical riches? Not merely possessions, which are really the least joyful of all gifts. But think of the gifts we are able to enjoy because of the physical makeup of our bodies. Through the riches of our senses—seeing, hearing, feeling, smelling, tasting—we are able to . . .

> *See the living masterpiece of a setting sun.*
> *Hear a precious little voice say "I love you Mommy."*
> *Feel a gentle breeze through barefoot toes on a summer day.*
> *Drink in the fragrance of lilacs on a twilight walk in early spring.*
> *Bite into a fresh-baked slice of homemade bread—dripping with butter, of course!*

What a treasure-trove is ours!

And still we haven't come to the end of His giving. He has created each of us with unique abilities. To some He has given musical talent. To others, a special artistic knack. To some, humor and wit. To others, the gift of hospitality. Some are especially good at working with children, decorating a home, or turning a house into a home.

If we are saying to ourselves, "Oh, no! Not me. I'm just an ordinary wife and mother. There's nothing special about me," we are neither acknowledging God's creative power within nor allowing Him to bring out our special talents. When we allow God to work within us, it is *He* who brings out that hidden gift. The seed of the gift is from Him. He knows best how to make it bloom.

God's giving doesn't end in us. If we try to keep His gifts to ourselves, we are robbed of their joy. The deepest satisfaction comes in giving them away. In so doing, we become links in a chain whereby God's giving continues on to others.

In the spiritual realm, our reflection of God's love and forgiveness must be offered to others in abundance. Strength, power, grace, glory, wisdom, knowledge, joy, loving-kindness, faith, and healing love are not for us alone. Through the Holy Spirit working in us, these gifts must be imparted daily to others.

"God has given each of you some special abilities; be sure to use them to help each other, passing on to others God's many kinds of blessings" (1 Peter 4:10 LB).

It is through giving that we receive, through the abundance of God's riches poured out upon us that we find true wealth . . . ever flowing from God to us, through us.

Dear Lord, we praise You for the wealth You have given us. Open our eyes today to the abundance of Your riches in our lives. May we lift our hearts in joyous song . . . knowing Your immeasurable giving has only begun.

amen

His Trustworthiness

Let my teaching fall like rain
and my words descend like dew,
like showers on new grass,
like abundant rain on tender plants.
*I will proclaim the name of the L*ORD*.*
Oh, praise the greatness of our God!
He is the Rock, his works are perfect,
and all his ways are just.

(Deuteronomy 32:2–4 NIV)

A mother comes equipped with an internal anxiety meter. It's right in the middle of her heart and has each child's name engraved on it. There are certain phrases in the English language that cause it to jump and spin . . .

"Mom, my teacher wants a conference with you right away!"
"Mom, remember how long Susie's hair used to be? We've been playing beauty parlor and . . ."
"Hello. This is the school nurse. We've been checking for head lice and . . ."

"Mom, Jamie's mother is on her way over and she looks mad!"

"Mom, remember the pretty flowers that used to be in front of Mr. Crabb's house? Here, these are for you . . ."

These are the standard meter spinners. We also have our family's encounters with each other, interaction with the neighbors, school friends, teachers, and others, not to mention the physical dangers our children are exposed to each day.

During the early years of their lives we nurture and prepare these little birds in the nest. Then it becomes time to let them try their wings in all kinds of new situations—social, emotional, physical, and even intellectual. As we watch these solo flights we are proud, but a little scared; hopeful, but a little apprehensive. We want to stand back and give them room to soar . . . but at the same time we want to hold their hands.

But we do release them into the world. And our anxiety meters begin to spin.

God has given us a natural and necessary protective instinct toward our children. But in today's mixed-up world these instincts can easily turn into fears. It seems our worries and anxieties increase in direct proportion to the grimness of the evening news or the vividness of our imaginations. Our hearts and minds are bombarded with scary situations, situations that could conceivably touch *our* children . . . and the meter goes on spinning.

Our anxieties are not limited to physical dangers, but extend to social encounters of the detrimental kind. The three "P's" of parental expectations can certainly cause a rapid rev of the ol' meter: academic *perfection,* social *popularity,* or athletic *prowess.* Dr. James Dobson says it best, "When the birth of a first-born child is imminent, his parents pray that he will be normal—that is 'average.' But from that moment on, average will not be good enough."[1]

Regardless of the causes of a mother's anxieties for her children, the potential is ever with us.

But the same God who gave us our children—these precious gifts of His love—is worthy and able to take care of them. *He is worthy of our complete trust.*

Trust: A conscious act of placing each child in His hands. With that act comes a beautiful awareness that through each experience—social, emotional, physical, and

[1]James Dobson, *Hide or Seek* (Old Tappan, N.J.: Revell, 1974), 34.

intellectual—He is at work in their lives. He is molding them into what He would have them become. Turning even what we perceive as hurtful into His good. Turning their failures—and ours—into footsteps . . . footsteps toward Himself.

Trust is the cornerstone of our relationship with God. All that He is to us . . . all that He has for us . . . is based on our trust in Him. Yet God is not diminished by our lack of trust, for His riches will continue to flow. But they will be like flood waters on hard, dry ground—unable to soak in and nourish the soil.

Whether in discord or disaster, we need to experience His deep and abiding peace. We need words of His tender mercies. Words of His supreme sovereignty over all of life's surprises. Words of His covenant power streaming through the ages. Words of His complete trustworthiness . . .

> Those who know your name will trust in you, for you, LORD, have never forsaken those who seek you.
>
> (Psalm 9:10 NIV)

> As for God, his way is perfect; the word of the LORD is flawless. He is a shield for all who take refuge in him.
>
> (2 Samuel 22:31 NIV)

> I [God] will maintain my love to him [David] forever, and my covenant with him will never fail. . . . But I will not take my love from him, nor will I ever betray my faithfulness. I will not violate my covenant or alter what my lips have uttered.
>
> (Psalm 89:28, 33–34 NIV)

> I will lead the blind by ways they have not known, along unfamiliar paths I will guide them; I will turn the darkness into light before them and make the rough places smooth. These are the things I will do; I will not forsake them.
>
> (Isaiah 42:16 NIV)

"Though the mountains be shaken and the hills be removed, yet my unfailing love for you will not be shaken nor my covenant of peace be removed," says the LORD, who has compassion on you.

(Isaiah 54:10 NIV)

I will betroth you to me forever; I will betroth you in righteousness and justice, in love and compassion. I will betroth you in faithfulness, and you will acknowledge the LORD.

(Hosea 2:19–20 NIV)

How minute my worries and concerns—even my biggest fears—seem in light of who God is. He is the sovereign ruler of heaven and earth. How can I imagine any circumstance in my life—or in the lives of my children—out of His control?

Sovereign ruler. Merciful and loving. What greater peace can there be than to know that we are bound—betrothed—to Him forever? There could be no more tender and loving bond than this. We are His beloved . . . each child of ours is His beloved!

Anxiety versus trust. It seems that a conscious choice is ours to make. Will we clutch our children to ourselves, fearful of what each day might bring? Or give them daily, even hourly, to Someone whose love for them is immensely stronger, wiser, and deeper than ours?

I prayed for this child, and the LORD has granted me what I asked of him. So now I give him to the LORD. For his whole life he will be given over to the Lord.

(1 Samuel 1:27–28 NIV)

It's time to unlock our hearts and remove the anxiety meter . . .

What meter?

It's gone!

Almighty Father, we praise You for Your eternal faithfulness. You are the Rock to which we can cling in every circumstance of our lives. We lift our children before You, knowing that with trust comes release. And with release comes peace. Not as the world gives . . . but a peace that comes only from You.

amen

His Grace

But he said to me, "My grace is sufficient for you, for my power is made perfect in weakness." Therefore I will boast all the more gladly about my weaknesses, so that Christ's power may rest on me.

(2 Corinthians 12:9 NIV)

Do you ever feel as though you are a total failure as a mother? Perhaps it is during one of those days when that impatient frown of motherhood seems frozen to your face? Or when you yell at the kids so loudly the windows rattle? Then, to top it off, after forty-two terrifying threats you still haven't meted out the discipline . . .

and the kids are still swinging gleefully from the chandelier.

It's always hard to come to God at the close of a day full of failure and frustration. We feel unworthy of the peace and rest He offers. Not only do we feel the pain of our imperfections, we sometimes feel doubt as well. We wonder whether we are acceptable to God. Surely He must be totally disgusted with us!

Feeling unacceptable, unlovable, and miserable we avoid fellowship with our Father. The next day we attempt to start with a "clean slate." We do all we can to earn God's approval (this can be a subconscious effort). We *will* be The Perfect Mother. Then we'll feel better, and our fellowship with God will be restored.

The day dawns bright and beautiful. The first sixty-seven minutes go fine. We smile and hum as we roust everyone out of bed for this wonderful new day.

And then . . .

The dressing dawdler begins her act.
Whining and bickering echo through the halls.
Doors slam.
Someone steps on the cat's tail.
Someone remembers the homework he or she forgot to do the night
*   before.*
The Perfect Mom loses her temper.
And her poise.
And her perfection.

A glare replaces the smile. Harsh words replace the hum. The veins in her neck bulge.

Sound familiar? We've blown it already and the day's barely begun. It can only go downhill from there.

When we come to the end of the day we're more discouraged than ever. The love and acceptance we tried to earn eluded us.

The cycle continues. We not only feel as if we failed our children, but maybe we've failed God, too. Despair and defeat move into our hearts.

Hey, wait a minute!

There is nothing we can do to earn His love and acceptance. He tells us, "I have loved you with an everlasting love" (Jeremiah 31:3). When we blow it, His feelings toward us don't change: "I am the Lord, I change not" (Malachi 3:6 KJV). If He loved us enough to sacrifice His son for us, nothing we do is going to diminish that love. "God demonstrates His own love toward us, in that while we were yet sinners, Christ died for us" (Romans 5:8).

We don't have to try to perfect our lives in order to come to Him and share His communion. In fact, it is during our times of failure and frustration that we need Him more desperately than ever.

He waits for us with arms open wide.
He waits beside the waters
      of grace and love
      of forgiveness and mercy
      of strength and guidance.
He waits for us to come—just as we are—and drink.

It is here we are set free from our fear of God's rejection and anger. There are no barriers between God and us—either real or imagined. The awareness of His love and acceptance frees us to respond to Him and to others with love.

Is it really possible to lead a victorious life with all the pressures and unforeseen calamities facing today's mother? Yes! The victory comes through an awareness of His unconditional acceptance and love: His grace!

As an example of His grace, have you ever noticed when dieting that it's easier to avoid temptation when you keep an attractive image of yourself in mind? If I think of myself as unattractive and hopelessly without willpower, chances are I will live up to my own expectations. Likewise, in my spiritual life, it's easier to avoid temptations such as impatience and anger if I keep an image of my acceptableness to God in mind. It's as if I am lifted above the circumstance and react in light of this saintly image. Because of my love for Him and the work of the Holy Spirit in me, my life begins to change into what I am in *His* sight—righteous and perfected because of the blood of Jesus.

As God's grace covers our lives it begins to touch the lives of others around us; not just because of the changes evident in our attitudes, but because we begin to feel the acceptance of God. It is then we can begin to openly love and accept others—just as they are. Especially our children.

A new awareness of God's grace doesn't change the circumstances that come into our lives. But the real change is in the grace with which we handle them. It is through this grace that we become victorious.

What a privilege to think we are leading our children to the fountain of His grace by showing them total, unconditional and beloved acceptance in our arms. Even as we remove them from the chandelier.

Blessed Lord, we praise You for the glory of Your grace which you bestowed on us in the Beloved. How can we begin to comprehend the depth of Your love for us . . . our preciousness to You—just as we are right now? Father, we are overwhelmed by Your grace.

amen

His Power

Ah Lord God! Behold, Thou hast made the heavens and the earth by Thy great power and by Thine outstretched arm! Nothing is too difficult for Thee. . . . Then the word of the LORD came to Jeremiah, saying, "Behold, I am the LORD, the God of all flesh; is anything too difficult for me?
(Jeremiah 32:17, 26–27)

Some of Creation's greatest evidences of God's power provided the stage for my childhood. His giant ponderosa pines were my playmates. His thundering waterfalls laughed and splashed into pools that tickled and numbed my toes. His sculptured domes of granite smiled down at me from the mountain peaks. His nighttime skies covered me with a glittering canopy of stars.

I was eight when I asked Jesus to come into my heart. In childlike wonderment I looked around and *knew* I belonged to a powerful God. Each time I lifted my eyes to the night heavens my heart agreed with the prophet Isaiah:

Lift your eyes and look to the heavens:
    Who created all these?
He who brings out the starry host one by one,

and calls them each by name.
Because of his great power and mighty strength,
   not one of them is missing.

(Isaiah 40:26 NIV)

When we consider Creation we can't help but wonder about the omnipotence of the God who brought it into being. All we see and know of His Creation was called into existence by His word. He created substance from *nothing*. Yet all the evidences of His power in our world are but a "veiling" of His real power.

God first revealed Himself as all-powerful to Abraham: "Now when Abram was ninety-nine years old, the Lord appeared to Abram and said to him, 'I am God Almighty [*El-Shaddai*]; Walk before Me, and be blameless [complete]' " (Genesis 17:1).

The promise God had given Abraham many years before was given again and was now about to happen—Abraham's posterity would become so large that he would actually become the "father of many nations." Kings would come from his lineage, and the land where he lived would be "an everlasting possession for this posterity." Abraham and Sarah had learned the futility of trying to accomplish God's plan in their own strength. They had experienced human insufficiency. But now that they were beyond the natural age of childbearing, Almighty God was going to overrule nature by performing a miracle. He would create new life—the promised seed—from within them.

Our God hasn't changed. The God of Creation, the God of Abraham, is the same yesterday, today, and forever. His power hasn't diminished. He is still *El-Shaddai,* Mighty Promiser and Giver of Gifts. All-sufficient. All-bountiful. Almighty God!

It blesses my heart to know I belong to a God such as this! But because I'm human . . . and busy . . . and have a mind occupied with four dozen other things at any given moment—I forget about His power.

I forget what He can do for *me.* I forget He has the power to change those areas in my life that desperately need His touch.

He has the power to help me overcome bad habits. And correct my wrong attitudes. And help me through an overwhelming struggle.

Sometimes I think my life is like my linen closet—constantly in need of cleaning, discarding, rearranging, and straightening. There are always a few undesirables that need to be discarded—gossip, yelling, gluttony, complaining, bitterness, fretting, jealousy, worry, pride, uncommitted struggles, IMPATIENCE—all jammed way back into the corners (*shudder*).

Unfortunately, linen closets never straighten or clean themselves. Likewise, we can't—*by our own power*—change our lives. We may try. I've been on more self-improvement campaigns than I care to remember, but these campaigns always seem to run out of energy. To bring about a permanent change of heart we need more power than our tired, human selves can muster.

Abraham and Sarah had to come to the end of themselves before God could show His power in their lives. We also must come to the end of our human resources (which doesn't take long for mothers!). We must realize our strength and determination alone can't do the job.

It is precisely at the point of our greatest weakness that His power is made perfect. Our Lord said, "My grace is sufficient for you, for my power is made perfect in weakness" (2 Corinthians 12:9). It is in our emptiness that we become filled with *His* power . . . the same power which raised Jesus from the dead!

> I pray also that the *eyes of your heart* may be enlightened in order that
> you may know the hope to which he has called you, the riches of his
> glorious inheritance in the saints, and *his incomparably great power for us*
> *who believe.* That power is like the working of his mighty strength, which
> he exerted in Christ when he raised him from the dead [italics mine].
>
> (Ephesians 1:18–20 NIV)

When we open the door and allow God's life-changing power to enter in . . . step by step, moment by moment . . . He begins a good work in us and will carry it on to completion until the day of Christ Jesus. Just as He overruled nature in the bodies of Abraham and Sarah to bring about the miracle of a new life, so He can perform miracles in *our* lives.

Deadwood is cut out. Discipline is applied. Priorities rearranged. In some areas He works quickly. In others, painfully slow. But His timing is perfect. And in precious awareness, He knows just how much we can bear.

Let's swing wide open those "closet doors" to our hearts and let *El-Shaddai* exert His resurrection power, tenderly cleaning and straightening our lives.

> *Dear Lord, as we look around us may we not only be mindful of Your awesome power in Creation—but also the greater power of changed lives. We praise You for this power . . . power that is perfected in our weakness. Thank You for loving us enough to want to manifest Your power in us.*
>
> *amen*

His Discipline

No discipline seems pleasant at the time, but painful. Later on, however, it produces a harvest of righteousness and peace for those who have been trained by it.

(Hebrews 12:11 NIV)

Most of us have had at least one week when everything seemed to go wrong. The kids knocked down the apple display at the market; the plumbing decided it was time to back up; the furnace died; the car had a flat (with the entire Brownie troop inside); and the stomach flu toppled the whole household.

These events don't always come in groups, but even one at a time they can be mildly irritating and sometimes downright exasperating.

A friend told me of one such exasperating moment at her house. Her husband was in the basement attempting to fix a plumbing problem. He was lying on the floor, disconnected pipes scattered around him, looking up into the problem area, when my friend decided to wash a load of dirty clothes. (These are the times that try men's souls—*and* marriages!)

Then there are the more serious events that enter our lives—seemingly without reason. The ones that slice at our very roots: perhaps a lost job; or maybe a transfer to another city—just when our hearts were becoming deeply embedded in a church home or community; maybe it's the extended illness of a family member; or a life-threatening accident; or not enough money to go around.

Do you ever wonder about the calamities that meet us head-on in everyday life? Do you ever ask as I do, "Why *me*, Lord?" Are daily catastrophes just happenstance or is there a reason behind them?

There is a story I love that helps me understand the events in my life:

> There once was a little seedling who lived on a tree farm on the edge of a sunny meadow. She was pale green and delicate—fresh from her seed in the dark, warm earth. Nourished and cared for by the Gardener, the little tree thrived and grew. She was protected from the harsh rays of the sun. No howling wind or slashing rain was allowed to touch her slender branches. Never was there a happier nor more content little tree. She loved her home and enjoyed the care of her Gardener.
>
> Then one day along came the Gardener with a large, sharp-edged shovel. He began to slice into the soil around her roots. The little tree trembled with fright and began to weep.
>
> "Don't cry, little tree," said the Gardener as he carried her deep into the forest, climbing to the summit of a barren slope. "You must be placed where the sun will blaze upon you and where the rains will drench your branches."
>
> "B-B-But, why?" asked the still-weeping little tree.
>
> "You have been sheltered, kept from attaining your full beauty and growth," answered the Gardener. "Now it is time for the searing of the hottest sun and the freezing snap of the coldest winter to bring you forth to perfection. The same rough wind that seeks to uproot you will be that which strengthens you to face the next."
>
> "I'm so afraid . . . " cried the seedling.
>
> "You feel pain and fear now, but there will come the day when your stunted form shall spring up into loveliness. You shall lift your strong branches and laugh in the sunshine."

I strongly identify with this little tree—do you? When the sweeping winds and searing sun hit my household, I cry and complain because I see these events with such short-sighted vision—I see only the circumstance with all its calamities. And soon I am caught up in a whirlwind of emotion as I worry about all the consequences and repercussions.

It is difficult to look beyond our circumstances to understand and accept what God is trying to accomplish in our lives. But James opens his book this way:

> Consider it pure joy, my brothers, whenever you face trials of many kinds, because you know that the testing of your faith develops perseverance. Perseverance must finish its work so that you may be mature and complete, not lacking anything.
>
> (James 1:2–4 NIV)

Pure joy? We can be pretty sure that James never had a two-year-old mark all over his new wallpaper with felt-tip pens, but I'm sure he understood very well the trials and testings of daily life. We *can* "consider it pure joy" to know that God treasures us enough to polish our rough edges. Looking beyond the frustrations, we have the assurance that His testings *are* bringing perseverance, and perseverance *is* bringing maturity.

"He disciplines us for our good, that we may share His holiness," (Hebrews 12:10). What a difference it makes in the atmosphere of our homes if we face those calamities with an attitude of joy. Not a fake, pasted-on joy—but a joy that comes from knowing that He is bringing us closer to a sharing of His holiness—through discipline.

So the next time those "rough winds that seek to uproot" sweep through our homes—let's rejoice! It won't be long until we can lift our hearts and laugh in His sunshine . . . in His holiness.

Maybe today.

Precious Father, Your discipline causes us to feel so treasured—like diamonds being cut and polished to Your perfection. Thank You for caring enough to use every circumstance in our lives to change us into Your image.

amen

50

His Beauty

Whatever is true,
Whatever is honorable,
Whatever is right,
Whatever is pure,
Whatever is lovely,
Whatever is of good repute,
If there is any excellence
And if anything worthy of praise,
Let your mind dwell on these things. . . .
And the God of peace shall be with you.

(Philippians 4:8–9)

My mother loves to tell of taking my three-year-old Melinda into a restroom that had been terribly neglected. In the midst of the scattered papertowels, dirty sinks, and leaking faucets, Melinda lifted her wide eyes to my mother and said, "Gama, I've never been in such a beautiful bafroom."

My mother was astounded. She suppressed a laugh and asked Melinda why she thought it was so beautiful.

"Because they play such pretty music," was the matter-of-fact reply.

Perhaps beauty *is* in the *eye* of the beholder. But I think it's more accurate to say it is in the heart of the beholder. We need to open our earth-bound eyes and behold our world with childlike wonder, looking beyond the blight of man's mistakes. Maybe then our hearts will begin to hear God's melody—rather than the worldly dissonance surrounding us.

God's artistic splendor is waiting for us to discover it. Sometimes it may be like searching for buried treasure . . . but it's there. Maybe a tiny violet peeking out from under some carelessly discarded trash. Or a hummingbird's nest hanging bravely from a rusty chainlink fence (complete with owner-architect resting inside).

Have you ever noticed that our attitudes and actions are contagious to those around us—especially our children? If we look for beauty—even in the midst of gloom or chaos—our children will subconsciously do the same. Conversely, if we look for the "ugly" in life (or simply ignore beauty)—sure enough—our little mimes will do the same. Alas, a new generation of complainers is born.

One hot summer Sunday morning, our family was trudging to a parking lot some distance from our church. I was commenting freely about the *horrible* smog and the *terrible* heat, when I noticed a young mother kneeling beside a weed-infested vacant lot. To my surprise she was inspecting a tiny daisy with her toddler. With unhurried care, she let him feel its soft coolness. He examined each petal and touched it to his nose. His happy eyes and her serene smile stayed with me a long time—so did a much-needed lesson.

But let's carry our treasure-hunt a little farther—what about the people we come in contact with each day? There are some whose beauty, both outward and inward, is obvious. And then there are the other ones. The ones with personalities that affect you like fingernails scraping a chalkboard. A co-worker, maybe? The PTA president? Your mother-in-law (gasp)? Sometimes we have to dig a little deeper to find that spark of hidden beauty.

When we find something beautiful in a person and treat them in light of it they actually become more attractive. Admiration will rejuvenate many a withering blossom.

Admiration works with children, too. If we look at them with *eyes expecting* to see beauty (not perfection) they'll try their best to live up to what we see in them.

Sometimes it takes an extra measure of faith to believe that beauty does truly reside somewhere inside. Especially in the face of a toddler's temper tantrum or a teen's rebellious outburst. It's helpful to keep in mind that God isn't finished with them. Just as a bud holds the promise of beauty to come—so does a child's life.

God has given me a never-ending reminder of His buds of promise. There is a tulip tree whose branches overhang our front patio. I believe it must be the messiest tree in God's Creation. Its leaves begin dropping on our patio in early summer and continue through the fall. When its branches are at last bare it suddenly develops large, hairy pods that begin dropping steadily (on our patio, of course).

Every January my husband threatens to topple this harbinger of patio clean-up. It is at this point that our exasperating tulip tree is nearly beyond any favorable comment and its beauty is certainly well-hidden.

But as we gaze up at its wiry network of branches we notice buds. Buds of promise. The ax is put away. We wait.

Nearly overnight, in early spring, our tulip tree joyously explodes into a lather of pink and white blossoms. We stand underneath it and rejoice at the wonder of God's artistry! Then we smile as we walk back into the house—being careful not to slip on the large, juicy petals that are already falling (on our patio).

We worship a God of beauty. His fingerprints are not limited to the obvious—the majestic splendor of the Grand Canyon . . . the energetic glory of Yosemite . . . the tranquil delight of Hawaii. His touch of beauty reaches every area of our lives. In Creation. In our peers. In our children. In us.

The choice to see it is ours. When we choose to look beyond the mundane, the drab, the irritating—a transformation begins within us. Attitudes change. Outlooks improve. We're pleasant—even fun—to be around. We've become (you guessed it!) beautiful.

> *We praise You, Father, for the reflection of Your beauty in our world . . . in others . . . and in ourselves. It is a gift of privilege and delight! What blessings of fresh wonder are ours!*
>
> *amen*

His Light

No longer will you have the sun for light by day,
Nor for brightness will the moon give you light;
But you will have the Lord for an everlasting light,
And your God for your glory.
Your sun will set no more,
Neither will your moon wane;
For you will have the Lord for an everlasting light,
And the days of your mourning will be finished.

(Isaiah 60:19–20)

There are some days in a mother's life when the sun just doesn't seem to rise. We may have been disappointed by someone. Or maybe we're not feeling good about ourselves or about our relationships with others. Maybe we're just lonely. Whatever the reason, a cloud settles in . . .

Usually this cloud of gloom brings with it a refusal to be cheered up. In fact, if anyone tries to cheer or uplift us we grudgingly summon a ghostly smile and slide back into our pit of despair—being sure to sprinkle a bit of guilt on the cheerer (usually our husbands) as we slither by.

This mood can almost be enjoyable. After all, our very lives are dedicated to the welfare of our husbands and children. Isn't it fun to let them know it—along with how wronged we've been—regardless of whether or not it's their fault? Poor us.

Does this sound familiar? I confess I am to some degree an authority on this subject. Alas, it comes from first-hand experience.

We are all affected by different circumstances. For some of us, something as simple as a cloudy day may touch off the blues. Fatigue often precedes them. Sometimes our depression is caused by someone who has spoken critically of us or a family member. The list is endless. The funny thing is that even when most of the reasons are legitimate, the resulting dejection isn't.

It would be depressing enough if we were the only ones affected by our dark days. But like it or not, we are the hubs of emotional stability in our families. If our outlook is sunny, it is reflected in every member of our household. If, however, clouds of self-pity, gloom, and despair hover over us, they also rain down on all who come near.

Even if we feebly attempt to disguise our negative feelings, those closest to us are never fooled. There is nothing worse than counterfeit peace, the "What's wrong, dear?"—"Nothing!" syndrome. The household remains shrouded with Mom's gloom.

The trouble with darkness is that it seems to be stronger . . . denser . . . and deeper . . . than light. We are almost fooled into believing that it is just as it seems.

But just as one small candle can dispel the darkness in an arena, so can the entrance of light into our souls dispel the bleak and dreary darkness lurking there. And how much greater that light—the light of the Lord—than one little candle . . .

> The Lord is my light and my salvation.
>
> (Psalm 27:1)
>
> For with Thee is the fountain of life;
> In Thy light we see light.
>
> (Psalm 36:9)
>
> Thou art my lamp, O Lord; And the
> Lord illumines my darkness.
>
> (2 Samuel 22:29)

Though I dwell in darkness, the Lord
is a light for me.

(Micah 7:8)

The Lord God is a sun . . .

(Psalm 84:11)

God's light is synonymous with His holiness and righteousness. Because He is light, darkness can't exist in Him. With His power and might, darkness has to flee wherever His light penetrates. With His light in our lives why should we ever be beset by darkness?

Sunlight can only be kept out by putting up barriers. It is the same with God's light. So it is wise to examine ourselves to see just what our barriers are. Self-pity? Anger? Hurt feelings? Rejection? These often are the culprits holding our soul's shutters closed to God's sunlight.

There are some steps that are sure to be successful for allowing our souls to once again bask in God's light. However, choosing to open ourselves to His sunlight can be difficult. It is a definite choice. It takes determination. *We* are the ones who must take that unsteady first step toward throwing open the shutters. So take a deep breath and step into the sunlight:

Give the entire circumstance to the Lord. Release it—give up your will to control it. "Cast all your anxiety on him because he cares for you" (1 Peter 5:7 NIV).

Confess areas of sin in your life and ask God to fill you with His light. "This is the message we have heard from him and declare to you: God is light; in him there is no darkness at all. If we claim to have fellowship with him yet walk in the darkness, we lie and do not live by the truth. But if we walk in the light, as he is in the light, we have fellowship with one another, and the blood of Jesus, his Son, purifies us from all sin" (1 John 1:5–9).

Ask forgiveness from your family and from others you have harmed with your bad attitudes. "Confess your sins to each other and pray for each other so that you may be healed. The prayer of a righteous man is powerful and effective" (James 5:16 NIV).

Immerse yourself in the healing balm of His Word. "If your law had not been my delight, I would have perished in my affliction. I will never forget your precepts, for by them you have preserved my life" (Psalm 119:92–93 NIV).

Praise God for His light in your life . . . and keep praising Him no matter how you feel. "Praise the LORD. Praise the LORD, O my soul. I will praise the LORD all my life; I will sing praise to my God as long as I live" (Psalm 146:1–2 NIV).

When dejection and low spirits threaten, return to God's Word (repeat last two steps). You can't trust your emotions only; trust Him. "Blessed is he whose help is the God of Jacob, whose hope is in the LORD his God" (Psalm 146:5 NIV).

God gave Noah a promise after the raging storm . . . the first rainbow, a symbol of His promise. God gives us a promise after the storm clouds roll out of our lives . . . another rainbow, the promise of His light in us.

This light doesn't end within us. Instead, our hearts become prisms for that light. When His pure white light streams into our lives and enters those prisms it bursts into a rainbow of joy, delight, gladness, and peace.

Just as sunlight streaming through a beveled glass window causes rainbows to dance around the room . . . so our rainbows dance on each person we're near.

We thank You, Lord, that You are our Father of lights. Our world grows sometimes too dark for us to bear. Yet Your light never changes, never grows dim, never wavers . . . How we praise You for that! Thank You for lifting us out of the darkness and into that light!

amen

His Word

> *But his delight is in the law of the LORD*
>   *and on his law he meditates day and night.*
> *He is like a tree planted by streams of water,*
>   *which yields its fruit in season*
> *and whose leaf does not wither.*
>   *Whatever he does prospers.*

> *(Psalm 1:2–3 NIV)*

Mothers need the thirst-quenching delights of God's Word. We need to lay back . . . let down our "roots" and soak up its nourishment. Truly, a wellspring of His riches will be our reward!

We've talked about the Bible being God's direct communication with us, bringing us knowledge of His character and, through that knowledge, comfort and nourishment in times of deepest need. But how about our need for practical instruction, for wisdom in ordinary day-to-day living—where a mother's body, soul, and spirit meet life head-on? How important is it to saturate our lives with meditation and thoughtful Bible study?

Let's look at Psalm 1 and examine the qualities of the tree whose roots reach deep into the streams of water and compare them to ourselves.

When I think of this tree I think of vitality. It is alive. Growing. Vibrant with good health. Vitality (or lack of it) colors its life, just as it does ours. Physical vitality is a sign of good health just as spiritual vitality—an energetic, optimistic attitude toward life—is a sign of a healthy spirit.

What causes this tree's vitality?

First of all, it is "firmly planted by streams of water." What security! It cannot be moved. Its taproot reaches deep into the clear, pure, ever-flowing river of life. It is sturdy and unbendable, and as its growth increases so does its capacity to take in more water.

It is a tree "which yields its fruit. . . ." It drinks vigorously from the life-giving stream and is fertile. Unhealthy trees can't bear healthy fruit. What fruit they may bear is small, shriveled, and bitter. Our fertility also depends on the health of our spirit, which in turn depends on the whereabouts of our taproot.

Some days I wonder why my spirit is not a clear witness to the Holy Spirit's presence in my life. Perhaps the fruit of the Spirit—love, joy, peace, patience, kindness, goodness, faithfulness, gentleness, self-control—are not readily flowing because of a displaced taproot. One that is busily shooting out in every direction—*except* deep into the ever-flowing Source (gulp).

This tree also has a natural sense of priority and order in its life—"it yields fruit *in its season.*" It does not drop its leaves, shoot out new growth, and bear fruit all at the same time. "There is an appointed time for everything. And there is a time for every event under heaven" (Ecclesiastes 3:1). We need to be patient with our growth, even our spiritual growth, and not expect perfection from ourselves at all times. Along the same line, neither should we overburden ourselves with too much work—even when it seems it all *has* to be done right now! After all, even God didn't create the world in one day.

"Its leaf does not wither." I would venture to guess that every mother in the world knows what it's like to wither. It may be because your four-year-old just yelled across the market, "Mommy, look at the funny-looking lady!" or simply because it's the end of a very long day. But if we are planted near streams of living water, our souls will not wither, even when our bodies are ready to.

"Whatever he does prospers." One of the definitions Webster's gives for *prosperity* is "a state of vigorous and healthy growth; well-being." Probably not the most popular definition according to modern standards. But what greater treasure could we ask for as wives and mothers—as women—than a vigorous growth in the knowledge of God's love and grace toward us?

How else can this knowledge be ours than by saturation in God's holy, living Word—a daily feasting at the banquet table He has prepared for us? A banquet providing vitality, security, fertility, order, endurance, prosperity . . . good health to our souls!

Because the pace of life today seldom lends itself to quiet times alone, we need to make a special effort to "attend the banquet table." God will honor this effort, this time spent reading, memorizing, and meditating on His Word. When we give Him a certain portion of our time He seems to "stretch" it and return it saturated with His influence. Our day seems filled with extra time. "Give, and it will be given to you; good measure, pressed down, shaken together, running over. . . ." (Luke 6:38). Do you think this could mean *time?* Hmm . . .

As with all God's abundant riches, this knowledge of God is not meant to be kept to ourselves. Part of the blessing comes in sharing it with others. As mothers we are doubly blessed to be able to share this treasure with our children, to teach them its preciousness.

> Fix these words of mine in your hearts and minds; tie them as symbols on your hands and bind them on your foreheads. Teach them to your children, talking about them when you sit at home and when you walk along the road, when you lie down and when you get up. Write them on the doorframes of your houses and on your gates, so that your days and the days of your children may be many. . . .
>
> (Deuteronomy 11:18–21 NIV)

Then shall our song—our declaration—be:

I rejoice in following your statutes
    as one rejoices in great riches.
I meditate on your precepts
    and consider your ways.
I delight in your decrees;

I will not neglect your word.

(Psalm 119:14–16)

Blessed Lord, we thank You for speaking to us through Your living, written Word. It seems we are nearest Your heart during the special moments we spend reading it. We praise You; we adore You for providing this precious treasure for us.

amen

His Order

. . . and the Spirit of God was moving over the surface of the waters.

(Genesis 1:2)

Twentieth-century motherhood can be the pits at times! The hours we spend as chauffeur, cook, confidant, and all-around-hub-of-the-wheel can leave our lives in tangled disarray. It is not surprising that the result of our hectic schedules is often complete chaos in our homes.

Kids under construction take an enormous amount of time, effort, and running around. And there is a lot to be said in favor of the merriment (and even mess) that comes with busy, productive, and formative activities. Often I find myself agreeing with the one who penned "Stop the world, I want to get off." It seems I'm always in a hurry. Rushing here. Rushing there. Enjoying the busyness, yet longing to slow down. Even stop. Hectic schedules forgotten.

How can we counteract this spin we're in? Must we drop the fun and productive activities in order to bring peace and orderliness into our homes? Or is the only solution to simply put up with a few years of disorder and disarray? There seems to be no other alternative . . . or *is* there?

Our God is a God of order. From the first chapter in Genesis to the last chapter of Revelation we see a plan. A pattern. A majestic sense of order. As a mom, I see no clearer evidence of order than in Jesus' life. One instance in particular is a startling example—the feeding of the five thousand (Mark 6:30–44). It teaches us some valuable lessons about the priorities of orderliness.

Jesus used a child. I've often wondered why Jesus chose to use a child's lunch? He could have created the food from another source—or from no source—after all, He created it in the first place. But He chose to use the resources of a small, poor boy.

Sometimes I find it difficult to use a child's limited abilities. When I'm in a hurry it's always easier (and faster) to do things myself. But that is a short-term, non-thinking, quick reaction to a situation. Think of what Jesus' act of involving the boy did for the child. Imagine how important he felt. His self-esteem must have grown dramatically that day. And what a wonderful opportunity to teach him the responsibility of sharing and loving others as himself. Certainly, the most important gift that day was not the one the child gave—his loaves and fishes, but the one he received—the joy that comes from obedience and giving, which entered his heart and stayed for a lifetime. How often, I wonder, have I robbed my children of their fragile self-esteem by insisting on doing something, simply for my own convenience, that they could do for themselves.

Jesus had a plan. He directed His disciples to have the people sit down in groups of fifty and one hundred so the food could be distributed quickly, efficiently, and fairly.

This makes me wonder what kind of pattern of organization I've established in my own household? Is there a direct line of authority and are there clearly defined responsibilities? What lifetime patterns are being established right now that will carry into the future?

Jesus used others to accomplish His plan. He certainly could have fed the multitude without any help, but He used human resources as well as His own supernatural power to accomplish His purpose. The disciples methodically carried out His instructions. Everyone had a job to do and they did it. There was no clamor or chaos. And when *everyone* had finished eating, Jesus had His disciples pick up the leftovers. Once again, each had his job to do and a sense of order prevailed. (Incidentally, this also implies that Jesus was concerned about waste—another pattern and principle to preserve.)

The order that was evidenced that day is a pattern we can use daily in our homes.

Chaos and order cannot co-exist. As we begin to organize, confusion recedes. Busyness still exists, but time is expanded when a plan, a pattern, and a sense of order take the place of disorder.

We need God's help in this area. We need to ask Him to rid us of our hesitancy to allow our children (through trial and much error) to take over more responsibilities day by day.

"But I don't have time to let them do it," you may groan. "It's so much easier to do it myself." That's probably true, at least initially. Teaching definitely takes more time than doing. But teaching lasts longer. Once you've taught your children to do things you've always had to do for them, time will be "stretched." As soon as they learn to do more for themselves and others their lives begin to blossom with new self-confidence. A sense of dignity and pride takes root as they learn to serve others in joyful obedience.

Chaos? Clamor? Disorder? Disarray? That's funny. It seems to have disappeared. Almost.

Heavenly Father, just as Your Spirit moved over the waters when the earth was without form . . . move over our homes and lives. Stir deep into our waters, creating order that can come only from You. Reign supreme over our time and our use of it. We will praise You in the new sense of calm and tranquility You have created in our homes.

amen

His Shelter

But I will sing of your strength,
 in the morning I will sing of your love;
for you are my fortress,
 my refuge in times of trouble.

(Psalm 59:16 NIV)

The storm howled. The wind-driven rain beat against the window. Jagged streaks of lightning cracked open the sky. Claps of thunder rattled the earth. Twenty-five-foot waves pounded nearby beaches. Tornados threatened to thread paths of destruction throughout the city.

That was outside. Inside was a different story.

We were warm. Dry. Snug. Gathered around the fireplace, we dug into a big bowl of warm and buttery popcorn. Laughing. Talking. Playing our favorite game.

The storm raged on, but we hardly noticed.

We were protected. We were sheltered.

That night I lay in bed listening to the rain outside my window. What a feeling of peace and security to hear the storm throwing its tantrum outside while I was resting inside, untouched by its fury. My mind drifted to the words of Isaiah: "A man shall be like an hiding place from the wind, and a covert from the tempest: like rivers of water in a dry place, like the shadow of a great rock in a weary land'' (Isaiah 32:2 KJV).

We have a hiding place from life's storms—the kind of storms that can wreak more havoc in our lives than the weather does to the landscape. Our hiding place, our shelter, is Jesus! Isn't it comforting to know that we (who spend so much of our time sheltering) have One to whom we can go for shelter? I like that!

Yet, notice that this verse doesn't say the wind suddenly disappeared . . . or the tempest subsided . . . or the river immediately transformed the desert into a tropical paradise.

I have often thought (and I am startled to realize this) that God's promise of shelter meant the storms would diminish, that the adverse conditions would disappear. When they haven't, I have thought that perhaps I wasn't whole-heartedly committing the stormy situation to the Lord. The resulting inner struggle would create more of a tempest than the one swirling on the outside.

God does choose to calm some of the storms in our lives. But others He allows to continue. There are certain situations that won't change for months or even years. Sometimes . . . never.

Some of us have children with physical or mental handicaps. Our hearts nearly break with compassion and concern for their little lives and what their futures hold. We stand by them, feeling every moment of pain and frustration they face. The storm clouds seem to gather again and again . . .

We may have a child who has a learning disability. The unending stress and hard work it takes to pull this child through his or her early years sometimes seems unbearable. The turbulence continues . . .

Your particular storm may be raising your children alone. Or maybe the chronic illness of a child (or yourself).

But, praise God! There is a shelter—a hiding place—right in the middle of the storm, in the eye of the hurricane. More than a place of brief respite from the storms of life, His shelter is a place where we can take up permanent residence. "The eternal God is a dwelling place, and underneath are the everlasting arms" (Deuteronomy 33:27).

Where is this dwelling place? Hidden, so that finding it requires an exhausting search? Must we dash around wildly in the midst of the raging storm? Where is this place of refuge and strength?

It is as simple—yet profound—as this: "We are the temple of the living God; just as God said, 'I will dwell in them and walk among them. . . .' " (2 Corinthians 6:16).

The God of all power and omniscience has chosen your heart and mine as His dwelling place. Isn't that a wonder? Because He dwells within us, the very place we need to go to be gathered into His sheltering arms is simply where we stand or sit this minute.

This shelter isn't meant to be an inner retreat from the world—or an escape from the realities of life, but rather a fortress that provides us with inner strength and stamina to face the storms. Immovable. Solid. Steadfast.

> God is our refuge and strength,
>   an ever-present help in trouble.
> Therefore we will not fear, though the earth give way
>   and the mountains fall into the heart of the sea,
> though its waters roar and foam
>   and the mountains quake with their surging.

(Psalm 46:1–3)

So let the tempests rage outside the windows of our souls. Let the world quake and crumble around us.

We'll hardly notice.

We are protected.

We are sheltered.

The Solid Rock abides within.

Father, we praise You for the deep and abiding peace of Your shelter. When life piles up in a heap we have You . . . our Refuge . . . our River . . . our Rock. We cling to You and praise You for the sanctuary of Your presence within us. How precious is Your comfort! How mighty is Your strength!

amen

His Strength

He gives strength to the weary
and increases the power of the weak. . . .
Those who hope in the LORD
will renew their strength.
They will soar on wings like eagles;
they will run and not grow weary,
they will walk and not be faint.

(Isaiah 40:29, 31 NIV)

There was once a young man named Icarus in Greek mythology who fashioned wings of wax and feathers in order to escape from an island prison. The wings worked great until he soared too close to the sun. Alas, the wax began to melt, and the feathers dropped off. Of course, it was curtains for the poor fellow. Such is life with wax wings . . .

As a mother I can identify with the need for wings. Ah, wouldn't it be glorious to actually take flight above it all! I can see it now—messy bedrooms, dirty bathrooms, hand-printed hall walls all far below me. Bickering, whining, and giggling kids left with mouths agape as I soar by.

Of course, Isaiah didn't mean God would issue us each a standard set of bird wings with which to escape our days. Rather he used picture language to express the wings born of deepest need.

Mothers through the ages have had a soul-deep need for strength. Wings of strength. Physical, emotional, and spiritual strength. For today. For tomorrow. Let's face it, the career we've chosen isn't an easy one. Some of us may have left rewarding jobs or careers outside the home in order to devote ourselves to the rearing of our children. Or maybe we expected something a little different than the twenty-four-hour-a-day working schedule of motherhood. No doubt about it—it's hard work! And often thankless (especially when we're *expecting* pats on the back).

It's no surprise that many moms begin to feel very alone—even isolated—by the housework, carpools, and unending tight schedules. Even if we've graduated from the diaper and baby-talk stage, emotional and physical weariness can still be with us. Add to this the push of women's lib and careerism. The weary mom finds it very easy to feel trapped by the very ones she loves the most.

We truly need God's strength to help us through these tiring and sometimes stressful days. Even more, we need Him to help us face the emotional challenge of being a wife and mother whose career is in the home.

With God's help, we can soar through our days on wings like eagles. We can soar with the soul-strengthening knowledge that He has chosen us for a very special role: We are molding tomorrow's citizens into the godly people He would have them to be. With His guidance, and our dedication to the privilege He has given us, truly "our sons in their youth will be like well-nurtured plants, and our daughters like pillars carved to adorn a palace" (Psalm 144:12 NIV). In light of eternity, can there be a more rewarding career than nurturing and developing these future members of God's kingdom?

God understands our weariness and has given us some special promises regarding our hours of dedication to our children. Each act of kindness we do—each glass of water we give our child, each potato we mash for his dinner, each load of little undies and socks we wash—will someday be rewarded. "And if, as my representatives, you give even a cup of cold water to a little child, you will surely be rewarded" (Matthew 10:42 LB).

In fact, as we accept each child as God's gift to us and dedicate our very lives to his or her well-being, it is as if we are doing it for Jesus Himself. "And any of you who welcomes a little child like this because you are mine, is welcoming me and caring for me'' (Matthew 18:5 LB).

What greater reward can there be, now . . . or ever?

In our modern society where *getting* often takes precedence over *giving,* it's hard to imagine the joy that can be ours in serving. Yet it is through serving others—our families, especially—that immeasurable riches are poured out upon us.

> If you give yourself to the hungry
>   [*making peanut-butter sandwiches?*]
> And satisfy the desire of the afflicted
>   [*with bandaids and kisses?*]
> Then your light will rise in darkness,
> And your gloom will become like midday.
> And the Lord will continually guide you,
> And satisfy your desire in scorched places,
> And give strength to your bones;
> And you will be like a watered garden,
> And a spring of water whose waters do not fail.
>
> (Isaiah 58:10–11)

It is through our giving that we receive. Springs of joy, gladness, guidance, nourishment, and strength are ours! When we lift our eyes past the duties and trials of our day—toward Him for whom we are doing them—our focus is changed. Thirst-quenching waters of joy flood our hearts. And it becomes true that . . . ''The joy of the Lord is [our] strength'' (Nehemiah 8:10). We will soar on wings like eagles. Wings of joy. Wings of strength.

> *Almighty Father, Renewer of our strength, truly our hope is in You. Even in our weariness we rejoice that every task we do is done as unto You. Thank You for giving us wings of strength that become stronger the closer we soar to You, our Source of strength.*
>
> *amen*

His Shield

Stand firm then, with the belt of truth buckled around your waist, with the breastplate of righteousness in place, and with your feet fitted with the readiness that comes from the gospel of peace. In addition to all this, take up the shield of faith, with which you can extinguish all the flaming arrows of the evil one.

(Ephesians 6:14–16)

As mothers, it certainly isn't hard to understand why the apostle Paul saw the need for armor. There are times when our homes seem like war zones. It may be an acute case of sibling rivalry that exploded into World War III . . . or simply "Astro-blitz" blaring from the home video game—but there is no doubt that mothers need armor (and earmuffs!).

Actually these kinds of wars aren't too difficult to handle—moms learn to exercise a great deal of shuttle diplomacy and become quite expert at peace negotiations. But there is another kind of war being fought in our homes. By an unseen enemy. An enemy who battles tirelessly for control of our lives and families.

For our struggle is not against flesh and blood, but against the rulers, against the powers, against the world forces of this darkness, against the spiritual forces of wickedness in the heavenly places.

(Ephesians 6:12)

Unfortunately our homes aren't in a demilitarized zone. Satan enjoys nothing better than to cause havoc in the midst of one of God's most sacred plans for us—the family. Statistics prove that Satan's darts have been very effective in ripping and tearing families apart.

He tries his best to slip his foot through the door. Then he lurks in the shadows . . . just waiting for a chance to trip us.

He knows that not only will his darts affect our Christian walk—but they will also influence the lives of our children (our watchers, our imitators). And of course, if he is successful, he can drive a wedge between husband and wife with some of his favorite tools: anger, nagging, bitterness, self-pity, and pride. (These are but a few at the top of his list!)

Yet, right on the battlefield where spiritual warfare wages day and night, God, in His mercy, hasn't left us defenseless. "Put on the full armor of God so that you can take your stand against the devil's schemes" (Ephesians 6:11 NIV).

Imagine, wrapped in the *full* armor of God . . .

Truth is our belt. Buckled around soul, mind, and body, it equips us with inner strength through a knowledge of God and His plan for us.

Righteousness is our breastplate. It shelters our heart—the center of our affections—with the righteousness of Christ. A mighty fortress Satan cannot penetrate!

Our feet are shod with the gospel of peace. We can walk through life with unwavering resolve and steadiness, protected from the stumbling stones Satan would plant along our paths.

In addition to all this, and even more necessary than all the others, is the shield of faith. We lift it before us to fend off any and all of Satan's darts . . . any and all of his temptations . . . victoriously!

I need a suit of armor like that! Do you?

Although the following excerpt is from a sermon written near the turn of the century, it was never more appropriate than it is today.

Paul wanted a shield, not against failure; that might come or stay away, but he wanted a shield against the pessimism that may be born of failure, and which holds the soul in the fierce bondage of an arctic winter.

Paul wanted a shield, not against injury; that might come or stay away; but against the deadly thing that is born of injury, even the foul offspring of revenge.

Paul wanted a shield, not against pain; that might come or might not come; he sought a shield against the spirit of murmuring which is so frequently born of pain, the deadly, deadening mood of complaint.

Paul wanted a shield, not against disappointment; that might come or might not come; but against the bitterness that is born of disappointment, the mood of cynicism which sours the milk of human kindness and perverts all the gentle currents of the soul.

Paul wanted a shield, not against difficulty; that might come or might not come; but against the fear that is born of difficulty, the cowardice and disloyalty which are so often bred of stupendous tasks.

Paul did not want a shield against success; that might come or might not come; but against the pride that is born of success, the deadly vanity and self-conceit which scorch the fair and gracious things of the soul as a prairie fire snaps up a homestead or a farm.

Paul did not want a shield against wealth; that might come or might not come; but against the materialism that is born of wealth, the deadly petrifying influence which turns flesh into stone, spirituality into benumbment, and which makes a soul unconscious of God and of eternity.

The apostle did not want a shield against any particular circumstance, but against every kind of circumstance, that in everything he might be defended against the fiery darts of the devil.

He found the shield he needed in a vital faith in Christ.[1]

We have the same defense. Our faith in the living God and in His beloved Son is our shield.

Satan's darts have no thrust, no power, in our homes or lives because we stand clothed in Jesus' righteousness ... redeemed, blameless, holy before God, who tells us ... "You need not fight in the battle; station yourselves, stand and see the salvation of the Lord on your behalf. Do not fear or be dismayed; tomorrow go out and face them, for the Lord is with you" (2 Chronicles 20:17).

Praise God! The battle's already been won (over two thousand years ago), and the victory is the Lord's . . . and ours.

Dear Lord, we thank You that even though the battle isn't over—it has been won! We take up Your armor and Your shield with praise and thanksgiving. We stand, knowing You are at our side, and claim victory in Your name. Indeed, You are a shield about us . . . our glory, and the One who lifts our heads! (Psalm 3:3).

amen

[1]John Henry Jowett, *The Best of John Henry Jowett,* (New York: Harper and Row), 42–43.

His Love

The LORD your God is with you,
he is mighty to save.
He will take great delight in you,
he will quiet you with his love,
he will rejoice over you with singing.

(Zephaniah 3:17 NIV)

In these writings we've touched on but a few of God's immeasurable riches for us. Woven together they cover our lives with a vivid tapestry of riches—with love being the shining thread interlocking each with the other.

God's love isn't just one of many of His riches, but the sustaining force behind them all. None of His other attributes would have any meaning without His deep and abiding, holy love toward us.

God loves us! What a glorious theme to wrap around our days! He loves us in our humanness, with all our weaknesses and imperfections, through all our mistakes and failures. In all that comprises twentieth-century motherhood, His love is the power that keeps our fragmented lives from flying apart.

The amazing thing is that He knows us completely, yet loves us totally. He knows us at our best; He knows us at our worst. Nothing about us can surprise Him; no discovery can disillusion Him. In fact, He sees worse things in us than we see in ourselves. But He continues to love us. What relief. What security. Nothing can quench His determination to love and bless us.

Think of the supreme value this gives us. We need never be ashamed of who we are or of what our occupation is. Our self-worth has no brighter crown than the knowledge that . . .

we are cherished and loved by the King of Kings and Lord of Lords!

In fact, God gave His only Son to die for us to secure a love realtionship with us. If love can be measured by how much the lover is willing to give (and it can be!) then there is no greater love than God's. He gave His own perfect Son as a sacrifice for us. He sent Him to suffer. To die in agony and shame. To take our punishment—the punishment we deserved—and bear God's wrath for our sins. Has there ever been a more costly gift?

> By this the love of God was manifested in us, that God has sent His only begotten Son into the world so that we might live through Him.
>
> (1 John 4:9)

> How can we comprehend . . . or even describe . . . such love?

> I can no more do justice to that awesome and wonder-filled theme than a child can grasp a star. Still, by reaching toward the star the child may call attention to it and even indicate the direction one must look to see it. So, as I stretch my heart toward the high, shining love of God, someone who has not before known about it may be encouraged to look up and have hope.[1]

Because of the nature of God's love He always desires the best for us: "He who did not spare His only Son, but gave Him up for us all—how will He not also, along with him, graciously give us all things? (Romans 8:32 NIV). Because He is the all-powerful, all-knowing, sovereign God who controls all things, He can accomplish His desire. Because of who our

[1]A. W. Tozer, *The Knowledge of the Holy,* (New York: Harper and Row), 105.

God is, His love is made perfect in His purpose for us. This is why there can be no fear in love.

If we think we are in the hands of chance, fear will reign. If we are looking for hope in the law of averages, fear will reign. If we are looking for our self-sufficiency to carry us through, fear will reign. And with good reason! But "there is no fear in love. . . . perfect love drives out fear, because fear has to do with punishment. The man who fears is not made perfect in love" (1 John 4:18 NIV).

So if our trust is in a beloved God whose love is all-powerful and perfect, how can we be tormented by fear? Love and fear cannot occupy the same heart. Everything (not just some things), *everything* that happens to us expresses God's love and comes as a furthering of God's purpose in our lives. God's love is in *every* moment of *every* day. Even when we don't understand why certain things happen to us, or seemingly "go wrong," we can rest (and rejoice) in the knowledge that God's love is in them and behind them.

God's love is holy and pure, never sentimental or indulgent. He isn't indifferent to our sin. His love can seem stern, for He is always (through discipline and redirection) changing us into what He wants us to be. Changing us into the image of His Son.

When we come to Jesus and acknowledge Him as our Lord and Savior, not only do we have God's outward love, but He literally *pours* His love into us through the person of the Holy Spirit: "The love of God has been poured out within our hearts through the Holy Spirit who was given to us" (Romans 5:5). What joy to know that we are such objects of God's love and delight! Imagine, our mighty God actually takes such great pleasure in us that He rejoices over us with singing (Zephaniah 3:17).

He sings a song of deep and tender joy, a song that has no beginning and can have no end. It is a song of love!

> *Beloved Father, we think about Your love with profound humbleness of heart. We can't earn such love and we certainly don't deserve it . . . yet You have poured Your love into our lives with an intensity that we can't even begin to grasp. Father, we bow before You in joyful silence!*
>
> *amen*

We Lift Our Praise!

I will exalt you, my God the King;
I will praise your name for ever and ever.
Every day I will praise you
and extol your name for ever and ever.
Great is the LORD and most worthy of praise;
his greatness no one can fathom.
One generation will commend your works to another;
they will tell of your mighty acts.
They will speak of the glorious splendor of your majesty,
and I will meditate on your wonderful works.
They will tell of the power of your awesome works,
and I will proclaim your great deeds.
They will celebrate your abundant goodness
and joyfully sing of your righteousness.
The LORD is gracious and compassionate,
slow to anger and rich in love.
The LORD is good to all;
he has compassion on all he has made.

All you have made will praise you, O LORD;
your saints will extol you.
They will tell of the glory of your kingdom
and speak of your might,
so that all men may know of your mighty acts
and the glorious splendor of your kingdom.
Your kingdom is an everlasting kingdom,
and your dominion endures through all genera-
tions.
The LORD is faithful to all his promises
and loving toward all he has made.
The LORD upholds all those who fall
and lifts up all who are bowed down.
The eyes of all look to you,
and you give them their food at the proper time.
You open your hand
and satisfy the desires of every living thing.
The LORD is righteous in all his ways
and loving toward all he has made.
The LORD is near to all who call on him,
to all who call on him in truth.
He fulfills the desires of those who fear him;
he hears their cry and saves them.
The LORD watches over all who love him,
but all the wicked he will destroy.
My mouth will speak in praise of the LORD.
Let every creature praise his holy name
for ever and ever.

(Psalm 145 NIV)

Our blessed Lord and Father, we lift our hearts in praise and adoration for who You are!

88

You are our Creator. All of heaven and earth was designed and made by You. The stars in their twinkling number are each called by name. The smallest sparrow is sheltered by Your hand. The thunder and crash of the greatest waterfall is but a glimpse of Your power displayed in Your Creation.

We know from the world You created that You are God all-powerful. We praise You for the same power You manifest in our lives because of who You are!

You are light. Holy and pure. We praise You for what this means in a world heaped to the brim with darkness and disaster. Your light is a beacon, an unwavering lamp—never dimming, ever glorious. Oh Lord, we need Your light in our lives.

Father, we are thankful that You are a God who changes not. You are now as You always have been and always will be. You are our Rock. Our Anchor! What security and peace that brings to our hearts. And all that You are to us will forever remain constant—Your faithfulness, Your purposes, Your promises.

Oh, how we rejoice that You are trustworthy. Because of Your character—unchanging and faithful—we can place our deepest trust in You. You will not fail us!

You are our sovereign God whose purpose in our lives is to bring us closer to Your heart. To love us. To bless us. To pour into us all the joy and delight our souls can hold.

Oh, blessed Father, we love You!

We love You for first loving us. For loving us with a love that searched us out and drew us into Your beloved arms. What comfort is ours to lay our heads against Your breast, knowing nothing can harm us. We are Yours! Nothing can separate us from Your love.

We praise You for Your omniscience. You know every detail of our lives . . . our yesterdays, todays, and tomorrows. You know our needs even better than we know them ourselves. You know our heartaches, our goals, our disappointments, our victories. Thank You for knowing and understanding . . . for being our mighty Counselor.

Thank You for being with us always. There isn't a place we can go that Your presence isn't with us. All that You are to us—Protector, Father, Friend—You are every hour, no matter where we happen to be.

We praise You for the riches of Your grace through Jesus, our Savior. Because of His atonement we stand redeemed in Your sight. Because grace closed the chasm between us we can reach out and touch Your hand. Where once we were sinners—You now call us friends! Oh, the precious gift of Your grace to us! Father, how can we describe how much we love You? Words fall so short of our heart's joyous praise!

Beloved Lord, when we behold You, our God . . . we are awed and humbled by who You are. When we see Your tender mercies toward us . . . we are awed and humbled by Your love for us.

When our hearts are lifted in an attitude of praise toward You, Lord, it's hard to concentrate on the drab or dreary in our lives. When we praise You, our thoughts—even our souls—are given wings. You fill our days with joy!

Father, may we learn the habit of praise. The necessity of praise. The delight of praise. For it is through our heart-response of praise and thanksgiving to You for who You are . . . for Your wellspring of riches . . . that our thirsty souls are filled to overflowing fullness.

> Therefore you will joyously draw water
> From the springs of salvation.
> And in that day you will say,
> Give thanks to the Lord!
>
> (Isaiah 12:3–4)